D1557453

PREPARE THE WAY OF THE LORD

Daily Reflections
On The Advent Season

Richard Gribble, CSC

CSS Publishing Company, Inc., Lima, Ohio

PREPARE THE WAY OF THE LORD

Scripture quotations are from the *New Revised Standard Version of the Bible*, copyright
1989 by the Division of Christian Education of the National Council of the Churches of
Christ in the USA. Used by permission.

Library of Congress Cataloging-in-Publication Data

Gribble, Richard.
    Prepare the way of the Lord : reflections on the Advent season / Richard Gribble.
        p.   cm.
    ISBN 0-7880-0850-1 (pbk.)
    1. Advent—Meditations. I. Title.
BV40.G75   1996
242'.33—dc20   96-10672
                                                                                    CIP

ISBN 0-7880-0850-1

Scripture speaks of the pearl of great price, that for which all is sold because of its great value. Friendship is such a great pearl for me. To my special and faith-filled friends, Mary, Laurie, Julie, and Jennifer, thanks for all the love you have shown to me.

Table Of Contents

Reflections For Christmas Day

Preface

We read in Isaiah the prophet, "A voice cries out: In the desert prepare the way of the Lord! Make straight in the wasteland a highway for our God! Every valley shall be filled in, every mountain and hill shall be made low: The rugged land shall be made a plain, the rough country a broad valley. Then the glory of the Lord shall be revealed, and all mankind shall see it together; for the mouth of the Lord has spoken" (40:3-5). Advent is a time of preparation, a time given to us by the Church to make ready our lives for the coming of the Lord. It is a special time which needs to be lived and celebrated.

We generally think of Advent as the time which precedes Christmas and thus prepares for Christ's coming in history. This is certainly true, but the season is twofold: a preparation for the Incarnation and for the Parousia, the Second Coming of the Lord. The preparations we make for these two events must be different. Christmas comes on a certain day which is known to all. Thus, we can prepare with the knowledge that we only need to be ready by the prescribed time. There is no great sense of urgency; we can procrastinate if we wish.

Preparation for the coming of Jesus at the end of time must by its nature be very different than our preparation for Christmas. This is an event which Scripture tells us will come, but we have no idea when it will occur. A greater sense of vigilance is required; we must always be ready. Our preparation for this event is ongoing, but in another sense it must be completed at the same time. Such a dilemma may create consternation or fear in some. Does each day that passes put us one step closer to our death or one step closer to the opportunity to see God? Attitudes will vary, but hopefully we look forward to the coming of the Lord, both in history and when history as we know it will terminate. The coming of the Lord can bring only joy for those who are prepared.

The Advent readings of the daily Eucharistic celebration provide much food for thought on these two questions. The lesser known theme, Jesus' Second Coming, dominates the first three weeks of the Advent preparation period. Only on December 17 do the readings shift dramatically in preparation for Jesus' birth. Preparation on both fronts is the theme and purpose of this liturgical season.

The reflections contained in this volume are intended to aid our mental preparation for Jesus. Centered about Isaiah's prophecy of "Prepare the way of the Lord," these short meditations reflect my understanding of the readings as communicated to me by God in prayer and reflection. Obviously each person will "see" different things in Scripture — such is its wealth for all of us. It is hoped that these reflections can serve as a starting point for your own prayer and meditation. Prayerful reading of the daily Scripture readings will certainly assist one to obtain the maximum benefit from what is written and shared in this collection. I hope that your Advent journey is filled with many blessings as you prepare your hearts and minds for the presence of Jesus who comes to our world.

Richard Gribble, CSC

Introduction

Something is happening — change is in the air; you can see it all around. The autumn leaves of gold, orange and red, dislodged from their branches by a gentle wind from the north, cover the ground. Squirrels, fattened with their coat of winter fur scurry about collecting the rich meat nuts. Some of these prize possessions will be buried in the earth and some collected in nests, all done so that food will be available in the spring. The duration and the strength of the sun begin to wane a bit more each day. Nature knows that it is time for change and preparation.

Society has become aware of its need to prepare as well. As the temperature outside has dropped and the seasons begin to shift, we too experience transition. We have exchanged short sleeves for long sleeves, short pants for long, cold drinks for hot drinks. We are more tired in the afternoon, reluctant to leave a warm bed in the morning, and retire earlier in the evening. All of these things are natural for us as humans.

Advent is the Christian world's time of preparation. In the midst of the reality of our places in the natural world we Christians are being warned to be alert, to be waiting, to be prepared. This is what the Church tells us during the Advent season. We need Advent — without it we stop being who we are, a people who are waiting. We need the Gospel's terrifying announcement of the end of time. We need the prophets' consolations and threats. We learn more about who we are in the uneasy raving of John the Baptist and in the gentle strength of Mary.

The barren leaves, the frost on the garden, the slow ebb of daylight — these are all warnings as sharp as the words of the Old

Testament prophets and as loud as the preaching of John the Baptist. We are asked to prepare the royal highway for the Sun of Justice, the Wonder Counselor, the God-Hero, the Prince of Peace. As Isaiah the prophet says, "Make straight in the wasteland a highway for our God! Every valley shall be filled in, every mountain and hill shall be made low; the rugged land shall be made a plain, the rough country, a broad valley" (40:3b-4). We need to build the superhighway to God by leveling the mountains of obstacles and filling in the valleys of barriers which keep us from our God.

In Advent our preparation is two-fold. We prepare for the Incarnation, Jesus' coming to our world in history. For this blessed event we prepare with time on our side. We know the date of his arrival and what must be accomplished before the event. Like nature we prepare systematically for what we know will come. At the same time Advent prepares us for the Second Coming. This event will come suddenly without warning. It will be a startling happening, like the twinkling of an eye or an unexpected snow that transforms the landscape. The image is proclaimed keenly in the Gospel warnings of the end of time, a terror made more frightening by the darkness of the receding sun and the chill of the evening moon. With Jeremiah we wail aloud, "The harvest has passed, the summer is at an end, and yet we are not safe!" (8:20)

Advent is the Church's winter, with its darkness and its cold, the threats of starvation, illness, and death. Yet, there is a paradox. In such a fearful night the lighting of candles brings great joy. In the numbness of silence the Spirit and the bride sing "come." It is the wondrous paradox of God's reign, where the desert blooms, the mountains are made low, where swords are beaten into plowshares, where the lofty city is made into dust, trampled by a nation of the needy and the poor. It is the paradox as well of a virgin found to be with child. It is our anticipation of Immanuel, God is with us.

Advent is a gift. Few people ever get the chance to prepare properly for things these days. We rush from one crisis to another; we never seem to catch up. The Church gives us Advent to prepare ourselves for the coming of the Lord. Effort is necessary to make our preparations efficacious, so that Jesus' coming will make a difference in our lives. May our endeavors be strengthened with the assistance of God. May the Advent season bring us to a greater sense of the presence of God as we prepare the way for the Lord!

Reflections
for
Advent

Isaiah 2:1-5
Matthew 8:5-11

Faith Leads
The Way

Life is a journey. Like all journeys it has a beginning, a middle, and an end. Our beginning is defined by our birth from a human mother into the world. The great middle of our life is lived out each day, from childhood through adulthood to old age. The journey of life, again like all journeys, has a goal. For Christians the goal is clear, union with God.

Within the journey of life there are many sub-journeys. Each has a beginning, a middle, and an end. There is the journey of formal education which begins with our first day in school and ends with graduation from our highest academic institution. There is the journey of marriage which begins with saying "I do" and ends with death. There is the journey of one's life's work which begins with our first formal job and ends with our retirement. Each one of these journeys has a goal whether it is an advanced degree, a golden anniversary or a particular position with the company.

Advent, the first season of the liturgical year, is a journey. It too, like all journeys, has a beginning, a middle, and an end. We began the journey yesterday with our Sunday celebration. The vast middle of the journey will be spent in our preparation for the Lord. The end will come when we celebrate Jesus' birth into human history, and his coming into our hearts and minds as well. There is a goal for our Advent journey. It is twofold — to prepare for the Lord at Christmas, and to wait with anticipation the Second Coming of the Lord. In short, our goal is to prepare ourselves to live in the house of the Lord.

Our readings today tell us about our Advent goal and suggest a means to achieve it. The beautiful imagery of Isaiah tells us that all nations will stream toward the mountain of the Lord's house. We are told to climb the mountain so that God may instruct us. This special instruction of God will bring peace to our world. Eventually, we will all walk in the light of the Lord. Our goal is to find the presence of God in our lives. We may have to climb mountains, figuratively or literally, to find our goal.

The Gospel suggests what is ultimately necessary to meet our goal and find the presence of God. Jesus says we must be people of faith. The Lord is amazed at the faith of the centurion, a Roman pagan who represented those despised by the Jews. Not in all of Israel has Jesus discovered such faith. It is faith which will return the servant to health and allow the centurion himself to climb the mountain and reach God's house.

The Advent season begins with a challenge. We are asked to make a sincere effort to adjust our lives, seek renewal and in general to climb the mountain to find God. In our society with its many outside activities which direct or focus our attention away from God, we will be forced to strive that much harder to secure our goal. Let us realize our need to reach God's house. Let us think what may be necessary to reach our goal. Let us use the faith given us by God to overcome the obstacles of society. May the Advent season be our vehicle in preparing our way for the coming of the Lord.

Isaiah 11:1-10
Luke 10:21-24

The Avenue Of Peace

A popular Christian hymn says, "Peace is flowing like a river." Today, with the situation in our world, one might logically think that the river has dried up, that it flows no longer. We might pessimistically think that peace has already passed us by and there is no chance for more. We see violence in our streets, schools, and our homes. The news each night is filled with reports which describe the lack of peace in our world. One might rightly ask, where is the Gospel, the "Good News" these days?

Contemporary times show peace to be somewhat elusive, but this does not mean that it is gone, has passed us by or stopped flowing. What is peace? Certainly it is much more than then absence of war. Peace must be an attitude, a way of living our lives. Peace is active. We cannot find peace by passively waiting for it to stop at our front door. As Pope Paul VI once stated, "If you want peace, work for justice." Peace must become our avenue of life.

Our readings today describe images of peace which are revealed to the merest children. The words of Isaiah ring with images of peaceful coexistence. The wolf will lie down with the lamb, the leopard with the kid. The calf and the lion will browse together and the child will play without danger near a cobra's den. This sense of peace comes from a shoot which will sprout from the stump, the family of Jesse. This one has wisdom, understanding, knowledge, strength, and fear of the Lord.

How can such peace, which seems impossible, be revealed? Jesus gives us some insight to an answer in the Gospel. God does not speak with the high and mighty of thought. The person of great intellect or position has no corner on the market of peace. In

17

fact, Jesus says that what has been hidden from the learned and the clever will be revealed to the merest children. In other words, Jesus gives a message of revelation, including the way of peace, to those who are open and ready to receive the word. Children are less cluttered in their minds and attitudes; they are more free and open. These are the ones who will be given the special revelation and message of God. God will reveal himself to those whom he wishes.

Peace may be elusive, but it can be manifest to the person who is open to the possibility of God. Peace does flow like a river, but as the words of the song also say, "It flows out of you and me." We must be the instruments of peace. It will be through our efforts that the beautiful images of Isaiah can become a reality. As we continue our preparation for the coming of the Lord, let us set our thoughts on what Saint Paul calls "the higher realms." Let us share God's peace with those we meet this day.

Feeding Each Other

There is an Asian tale which describes the difference between heaven and hell. The image of hell is this: There is a large banquet table. This table is adorned with all the finest that a person can imagine. The tablecloth is pure white silk; the finest china is being used. There is even a beautiful silver tea service that is present. The finest food and drink are being served as well. The guests are all dressed in their best clothes. There is only one thing that seems out of place. The utensils present on the table are very large, so large, in fact, that one person cannot use them. In the process of trying to eat the meal before them the guests bump into each other and arguments break out. In the end no one gets anything to eat; all remain wanting and unsatisfied.

The image of heaven begins in the same way. There is the same great banquet table with all the finest in china, food, and associated decorations. The same large utensils are present. There is a different set of guests that have been invited. These people realize that the utensils cannot be used by one person, thus they begin to help each other. Because the people have learned to feed one another all are filled and satisfied.

In our readings today we hear about how God provides for us, and our need in turn to feed each other with the bounty provided by God. The book of Isaiah is filled with metaphors, many of which we hear in our Advent readings. Today's reading does not disappoint in this way. We are told that God will provide for us a banquet of the choicest food and drink. But we hear more. God is the one who destroys the veil that shadows all people. God is the one who wipes away all tears; God will destroy death forever.

In the Gospel we hear a familiar story. Jesus feeds those who have been listening to him and are weary from hunger. God again provides the great bounty. It is important to note, however, that Jesus asks the disciples, his closest followers, to distribute the food to the people. These friends of Jesus are thus asked to feed others.

In our lives we have been provided with an abundance. It comes in the form of food and drink, family, friends, loved ones, and material possessions. We just celebrated the great bounty which God has given to us in our annual Thanksgiving feast. Now we need to go one step further. We need to take the bounty and use it to feed others. We feed others in the work and ministry that we perform. Many are benefitted and fed by what we do. Do we equally feed those who are most dear, the closest people in our lives? We have all known people who have shown us by their lives how to feed others. They have become servants and witnesses of God's love. Such people have taken seriously Jesus' edict that he came not to be served, but to serve, to offer his life as a ransom for the many. Such people touch our lives and draw us closer to God by their faithfulness to the call of the Lord.

Advent calls us to review the life we live and adjust accordingly. In waiting for the coming of the Lord we are challenged to see how we can better use the bounty of God in feeding others. Through our service and example we have the opportunity of drawing others closer to the Lord. Let us work together to aid others. Let us feed our brothers and sisters and in the end find eternal life!

Isaiah 26:1-6
Matthew 7:21, 24-27

God: The
Anchor Of All Life

If you have ever been on a ship at sea, especially during a storm, you know the power of the ocean. The waves, wind, rain, and swells create a frightening scene, especially to one not initiated into such a situation. Large ships are tossed about like toys in such conditions. If a ship is near shoal water and thus in danger of running aground, a wise captain will give the order to "let go" the anchor. An anchor is solid, heavy, something that seems strong and permanent. In order to be effective, however, an anchor must find an equally strong and permanent fixture upon which to attach itself. If the anchor runs along a sandy ocean bottom it will not be able to hold the vessel from drifting into danger. If the anchor finds a rock, however, then the drift of the ship can be checked. Without the anchor and its mating with the rock, a ship will travel "in harm's way."

Today's readings speak of Jesus as the foundation, the rock of our life and our need to anchor ourselves in him. Isaiah gives us another metaphor today. We are told to trust in the Lord, for the Lord is an eternal rock. God, the rock, humbles those in high places and brings the lofty down to the level of the dust.

The Gospel shows us how we are to use this rock which is our God. Jesus uses the analogy of a house built on rocky or sandy ground to make his point clear. The Lord says that if we build our house on rock it will be safe. Houses built on sandy soil will be imperiled. Jesus himself is using a metaphor to teach an important lesson on where our foundation must be. The house is our life. If we center our life on the rock, that is Jesus, then when the storms of this life, the problems, illnesses, deaths, and other unexpected happenings occur, we will be able to weather them. Conversely, if we build our life on the sandy soil and neglect the rock, which is Jesus, then when the destructive storms come our life will be shaken from its foundation and may be totally lost.

There are several images of rock which are popular in today's society. One insurance company says that you are safe if you have a "piece of the rock." Jesus, we remember, called Peter the rock. Why? Because Peter was to be the foundation and strength, the bedrock, of the fledgling community which was the Church.

We must anchor ourselves in the rock which is Jesus. The symbol of my religious community, the Congregation of Holy Cross, is a cross with two anchors at its base. The Latin words *spes unica*, (only hope) tell us that our one and only hope must be placed in the rock, Jesus, and in his cross. This, of course, will lead us to death, but we will also experience resurrection and eternal life.

Advent allows us the opportunity to determine what adjustments are necessary in our life. As we wait for the Lord's coming let us never fail to remember our need to anchor ourselves in God and especially God's son Jesus, the one who is our refuge, our strength and ultimately our source of everlasting life.

Seeing God Through Faith

Anne Sullivan truly was a miracle worker. In the late nineteenth century she was working as a teacher of the blind and deaf. Her special talents would be tested severely when she met a young girl named Helen Keller. Helen had been left deaf, dumb, and blind as a result of an early childhood illness. Anne Sullivan was called upon to break through the silence and the darkness which were Helen's life. First, Helen had to learn that there was a possibility for something other than the environment she now knew. Helen Keller had to develop faith in Anne Sullivan's ability to lead her to a future which was more than silence and darkness.

When Helen made the turn in her life and began to believe in the possibilities the future held, then she was on the road to a new way of life. Helen Keller never again was able physically to see. She was never again able physically to hear. But with the faith which she developed she was able to break through her isolation and find a whole new world of possibilities which would mean for her a new lease on life.

In our readings we hear two different accounts of the blind able to see through the gift of faith. Isaiah says that God will open the eyes of the blind and the ears of the deaf. These things will happen because God desires to raise the lowly and bring them joy.

In the Gospel account Jesus encounters two men who are physically blind. They are not, however, spiritually blind. Jesus asks, "Are you confident I can do this?" The confidence and faith showed by the two men is rewarded. Now they are able to see, both physically and spiritually.

Most people are able to see and thus to enjoy God's creation. At times, however, we do become spiritually blind. There are occasions when we make little effort to recognize the presence of God in others, in events, and in the general busy nature which is our daily lot in contemporary society. Sometimes God calls us and we do not stop; we do not recognize God. The call can come in the form of an interruption; it can come in the form of an unexpected event. God comes many times when we least expect his presence. Thus, we must be ready and vigilant to grasp the opportunity which God's presence affords us.

Advent can be a wonderful time to slow down a bit, pause and reflect on the presence of God in our life. This can only happen, however, if we will allow it. Society is so geared toward the Christmas celebration that Advent is many times bypassed with hardly a thought. Let us this day make a conscious effort to slow ourselves down, to open our eyes so as to recognize the presence of God in our lives. Let us allow the Advent spirit of anticipation and preparation to blossom forth in our efforts to find God this day.

Isaiah 30:19-21, 23-26
Matthew 9:35—10:1, 6-8

Pass On
The Gift

Could you imagine giving away twelve million dollars? That is exactly what Katharine Drexel, foundress of the Sisters of the Blessed Sacrament for Indians and Colored People, did. Katharine was the heiress, along with her two sisters, to a fortune accumulated in the field of banking by their father, Francis A. Drexel. Katharine had used her inheritance for her own benefit as well. She received a fine education and was well traveled in her youth. She realized, however, from her strong Christian foundations, that all was a gift from God and thus should be shared. She wanted to pass on what had been given to her.

Katharine's Drexel's religious community has been responsible for many great works, courtesy of the money that she gave and the hard work of her co-religious women. Indian mission schools were established in Arizona and New Mexico. Xavier University in New Orleans was founded by Mother Katharine's community of sisters. God had provided an abundance and Katharine Drexel made the conscious decision to pass it on.

In our readings we hear about all of the many good gifts given us by God and our need to pass them along. Isaiah, in his usual beautiful imagery, speaks of the food and drink which will be provided. Instruction on the proper road in life to follow will be given. Rain will water the land and the harvest in turn will be abundant. Light will brighten the earth seven times greater than normal. The wounds of the injured will be bound up and healed. God is the one who will provide all these wonderful gifts.

Jesus suggests in the Gospel that we must pass on the abundance given to us. The Lord himself provides for us with the teaching of the good news and the curing of all ills. Jesus goes one step further, however, and says that workers must be sent to the harvest; the gifts of God must be passed along to others. Jesus sent the first laborers, the apostles, to preach the word and to serve others. He gave them, as we hear in the Gospel, the gifts to cure sickness and disease of every kind. The Lord told them to share what they had been given: "The gift you have received, give as a gift."

I am not sure when I first heard it, but the expression "pass it on" has made a powerful impression in my life. We have all been given much — now it is time to pass it on. We have been given material possessions. At this season it is normal to see people share and open their hearts and pocketbooks more generously. This, however, must be the norm for our life. It should not take Advent to precipitate such action. We have been given the gift of our minds and, for many of us, the opportunity to receive a good education. Can we now share this gift with those who need special help in understanding the many complex ideas in our society? We have been given time and opportunity. Are we ready and open to share these gifts as well?

God has provided all good gifts, our very lives, material needs, our faith. God gave us Jesus, the one whom we await during this special season, to show us the way. Let us share what we have and who we are with those whom God has given us to love, nurture and assist. Let us pass on the gift this day!

God Will
Save Us

Many years ago my father, brother-in-law, and I were involved in a discussion about our various experiences in the business world. My brother-in-law was sharing many facts and figures about stocks, bonds, and interest rates. My father was listening and countering some of what was being said with different data. In the midst of the discussion my brother-in-law's four-year-daughter came up and asked my father, "Papa, are you discussing a matter of economics?"

I remember that story because of its humor, but also because of the insightfulness shown, even by accident, by a little four-year-old girl. Whether she knew it or not, she had understood the point of the discussion. She was able to make the proper connections in what was being said to come to a logical conclusion. My niece was able to relate one thing to another so as to achieve a proper understanding.

In the Gospel today, it is evident that the scribes and Pharisees, unlike my niece, do not get the point of Jesus' words and actions. They are not able to make proper connections and, thus, do not understand what message is being proclaimed. The Jewish leaders are not able to see that there can be a connection between sin and paralysis. The point is not that the paralytic may have been a sinner. Rather, Jesus is trying to show the scribes and Pharisees that sin is a form of paralysis. It weighs us down. With the removal of sin, as in the case of the cure of the paralytic, one is able to walk again, free and unencumbered.

We are many times held down, made to feel as if we are paralyzed by sin. All of us have felt the burden of sin. When we are not as close to the Lord as we wish, the journey of Advent becomes quite difficult. At times the burden seems so great that we are unable to walk, to maintain proper direction in our lives. Sin can paralyze our thought as well. Our conscience becomes tied up in a knot when we do not follow its direction. We can become confused. In a figurative way we have become paralyzed; we cannot function the way we wish or know we can.

Advent is a time for renewal as we prepare the way for the Lord. Reconciliation allows us to be renewed in our relationship with God and with one another; it allows us to remove the burden of sin which may exist. We must realize our personal brokenness and, thus, our need for the reunification which reconciliation provides. Next we must see the need to forgive and be forgiven by others. Lastly, our need for reunion with God calls us to seek reconciliation with our Creator, the source of all good. In short, we need to break the web which veils us and does not allow us to be who we need and want to be.

The new life which we seek can be seen in many ways. As we have seen throughout this season, Isaiah provides the proper image for the message of Scripture. The prophet speaks of how the desert and parched land will exult. Streams will burst forth in the desert; the burning sands will be made pools. The thirsty ground will become a spring of water.

All these images of renewed life show us how God will remove our burdens and save us, if we will only allow God to act. During this season of preparation and waiting we are challenged to make the proper connections, to get the right point in our relationship with God. We have our faith; we have a process of reconciliation. Let us seek God and blossom forth armed with the sure knowledge that God will save us. The gift we will receive is eternal life.

Remove The Barriers To Love

I fled Him, down the night and down the days;
I fled Him, down the arches of the years;
I fled Him, down the labyrinthine ways
Of my own mind; and in the midst of tears
I hid from Him, and under running laughter.
Up vistaed hopes I sped;
And shot, precipitated,
Adown Titantic glooms of chasmed fears,
From those strong Feet that followed, followed after.
But with unhurrying chase,
And unperturbed pace,
Deliberate speed, majestic instancy,
They beat — and a Voice beat
More instant than the Feet —
"All things betray thee, who betrayest Me."

So begins Francis Thompson's famous poem, *The Hound of Heaven*. In the poem the hound, who is our God, is in a constant search for the lost and forsaken. We cannot hide from God; we cannot escape God's search. There is no barrier, hurdle or obstacle that is too high or difficult for God. All barriers will be negotiated by our God in the quest for humankind.

Our readings today speak about how God pursues us, removing barriers, and our need, in turn, to remove obstacles which keep us from God. In a certain sense the action of the shepherd in the Gospel makes no sense. What logical person would leave 99 perfectly fine sheep alone so as to search for the one who has strayed? By any contemporary standard, 99 percent is good and in school receives a grade of A. God, however, is not always logical from a human perspective. God will always go after the one that is lost. Those present do not need the shepherd as does the one who is lost. There is no person who will be forgotten by God.

We know that barriers exist that make the search for God more difficult. Isaiah speaks of how the barriers must be removed. The image of a great highway in the desert is used to make ready the way of the Lord. In order for this highway to be built, however, the valleys must be filled in and the mountains leveled off. The rough ways must be made smooth. Only then will a good path exist for the meeting of God and God's people.

It is unfortunate but true that many barriers exist in our life which keep us from being the people who God asks us to be. These barriers keep us from being people of love toward ourselves, others, and God. One obstacle that many times plagues us is our attitude. How many times have we put another person at a distance simply because that person is different than we are? The person may speak another language, have another color skin, think differently than we do or come from another country. The Lord says we must remove all obstacles which come between us and our ability to love others.

Sometimes the obstacles are more internal. We think that we are not smart enough, attractive enough, that no one could possibly love us. We get down on ourselves; our self-esteem is low. We must realize, however, that the bumper sticker which says "God doesn't make any junk" is true. We are God's greatest creation. Made in God's image and likeness we certainly are good and important; we can be and are loved by many people.

Barriers also exist in our relationship with God. Material things, such as the car, the house, our clothes, the television and VCR, can get between ourselves and God. When this happens, then our priorities are askew and the created world is worshiped and the Creator is ignored. At times our work comes between ourselves and God. As well intentioned as we may be, there are times we become so wrapped up with what we do that we forget that the talents we possess and the opportunities given to work come from God. It is true as well that at times our own idea of self-importance comes between ourselves and God. Jesus says that we must remove all barriers that come between us and our ability to love.

During this Advent season we have the opportunity to renew our relationship with God, as we await the Lord's coming in history and prepare for his return at the end of time. Let us, therefore, search our hearts and minds for any obstacles which may exist in our lives. Let us remove all barriers that keep us from our ability to love ourselves, others, and ultimately God and God's son Jesus, our refuge, our strength, and our source of eternal life.

God Is The Source Of Our Strength

Contemporary life is filled with challenges, at home, in the work place, in the community and within the Church. At home parents are daily challenged in the duty of raising their children with Christian values. Spouses are challenged to love at all times, despite the anxieties, problems, and difficulties of life. Families are challenged to find ways to maintain themselves as a unit and to avoid influences which break down their mutual love.

We face challenges at work each day. How do we do ten things at once and do all of them well? We are faced with the reality that it is important to get ahead, but how can we do it without stepping on the rights of others? Workers are asked to please their supervisors and supervisors are tasked with the responsibility of the maintenance of company spirit — both are daily challenges.

The community in which we live also presents us with challenges in our daily routine. Neighborhood watch programs exist to keep homes secure and residents safe. It is a challenge to build a true community for organization and action. Assistance must be rendered to others, especially those who are less fortunate, with time we do not have.

The Church presents us with many challenges as well. We are called to be evangelists and spread God's word. We need not stand on a street corner and wave the Bible, but we must bring others closer to God by our words and actions in our daily lives. We are also challenged to do our fair share of God's work in our parish. All are called by their baptism to serve and minister in the community of faith.

All of these challenges, at home, in the work place, in the community, and with the Church, cause us to grow weary. As humans we are finite; we can only give so much. We need to be refueled periodically, given food for the journey and the trials that will come in the future.

Our readings today show us that God must be the one to whom we turn for our fuel, that which feeds us in our lives. Isaiah says that God never grows weary or faint. We know that God is all powerful. God, therefore, gives strength to those who are faint; in the weak God makes vigor abound. Those who place their hope in the Lord will be renewed in strength; they will soar as on eagles' wings. In the Gospel Jesus invites the weary and those with burdens to come to him. Jesus will refresh us; our souls will find rest.

We know that our lives cannot escape weariness and burdens. But where do we turn to find refuge from this onslaught of reality? The world in which we live is a tough place. As they say, "there is no such thing as a free lunch." The condition of our world, what some theologians call the "original sin," is the common lot for all. The world gives many answers to the dilemma of our weariness and burdens. Some answers, such as drugs and alcohol, are no solutions at all, but rather are an escape from reality. Some temporary solutions are proposed; some solutions skirt the problem, brush it under the rug or fail to deal with it.

The refrain to a popular hymn says, "Only in God will my soul be at rest, from him comes my hope, my salvation. He alone is my rock of safety, my strength, my glory, my God." God alone is the one who can provide the strength we need and the solutions we seek to the challenges and problems we face. God's answer might not come tomorrow, but then God does not operate on our time table.

Our preparation for the coming of the Lord must include the placement of our complete trust in the Lord's abiding love and presence. God alone gives rest to the weary, gathers the wayward and reconciles the sinner. Let us find our strength in God this day!

Isaiah 41:13-20
Matthew 11:11-15

Accepting God Brings Life

In 1977 Oscar Romero became the archbishop of San Salvador in Central America. Romero was chosen, most probably, because of his conservative background. He was a man of books and education; he was a man of the academic life. The rich citizens of the region were happy with his selection. They felt that he would pursue their agenda and thus allow a privileged minority to dominate the Church and society.

Oscar Romero, however, began to listen to the cries of his people, dominated by the poor working classes. Romero's ability to listen transformed itself into action on behalf of those who had little or no voice. The archbishop spoke out against injustice and worked to bring greater freedom and more humane rights to the people of his land. His change of attitude and heart angered many in the government. He became a marked man for what he believed and taught. Oscar Romero's openness to transformation, and consequently his ability to listen to the people, made him a prophet in his day. His acceptance of God's call in his life produced life.

Although Archbishop Romero was felled by an assassin's bullet in 1980, his memory and work continue to influence many. By his life many of the people of Central America have been empowered to bring the cause of human rights to the forefront. People throughout the region and the world experience better conditions because of one man's courage and acceptance of God's plan in his life.

Our readings today speak of how life can be drawn from our acceptance of God. In the Gospel we hear for the first time this season of John the Baptist. God sent John to prepare the way for

34

the Lord. His message was simple and direct — the people needed to change. Jesus in the Gospel speaks of the greatness of John. The people would not listen to him. Thus, they missed the opportunity to recognize the face of God in Jesus, the one to whom John pointed in his ministry.

If the people had recognized God all possibilities would be present. In the first reading Isaiah speaks of how God will help the people. God will answer the needy and the afflicted. God will turn the desert into marsh; the dry ground will spring forth with water. Trees will be planted in the desert. In short, God will bring life to those who accept his way and message.

God's messenger comes to us, but many times we miss the message, the person, and the opportunity. In this we miss the possibilities which life can bring. Messengers come in many forms. There are the Oscar Romeros of this world who challenge us by preaching God's word. The poor can also speak to us from their economic and social plight. God's message is given to us by the child and the spouse. We must recognize God's presence in these messengers; we must listen and act. We must prepare our hearts for the coming of the Lord. If we do not, then certainly God will pass us by and we will miss the opportunity of a lifetime. Let us this day open our hearts, ears, eyes, and minds to the possibility of God. Let us prepare the way of the Lord and in the process find eternal life.

Isaiah 48:17-19
Matthew 11:16-19

Follow The Signs
That Lead To God

Signs provide us with lots of information. You cannot go very far these days without seeing a billboard. Such signs tell us of upcoming events, restaurants or motels down the road, as well as the latest in fashion, sales and products. One cannot get into a car without encountering many street signs. These signs tell us how far to our destination, they provide warnings about obstacles ahead, and they inform us of the rules to be followed in order to safely proceed on the highway. The weather can also provide certain signs. Anyone who has been in the navy knows the expression, "red sky in the morning, sailor take warning; red sky at night, sailor's delight." People today talk a lot about the "signs of the times." An economic depression, violence in the streets, countries at war — all of these are signs of the contemporary scene. They tell us something about the direction of our society and world. All of the signs that come to us are only useful if we follow them. Signs provide direction in our life, leading to certain goals or objectives.

Our readings today speak of the direction given us by God and its rejection by God's people. The Hebrew Scriptures are replete with incidents of how the people of Israel failed to heed the directions given by God. The prophets were sent to give the people God's message, the direction in which they needed to go. Isaiah, from whom we hear this day, as well as many other prophets, tells the story of the Hebrews as they sometimes followed and other times rejected the direction given them by God. Isaiah tells us today that if the people would listen to God's voice, then they will be provided with all they need.

Today's Gospel, like yesterday's reading, tells us about John the Baptist. Although Jesus extolled John, we hear that the people acted like little children in their reaction to John's message. They saw him as crazy; they did not listen to his words. In failing to listen and heed John's warning, his signs and direction, the people were not able to recognize the presence of God in Jesus. John provided the way, but it was not followed.

We are provided with many signs of God's presence. Some of these signs we accept and recognize; others we see but fail to recognize as God's presence. Others, unfortunately, we ignore all together. Preparation requires our attention; we need to be open to God's presence. We must heed the signs which show us the correct path, the way that leads to life. Let our preparation for the coming of the Lord continue by looking for God's presence in the many ways God is manifest to us, today and each day of our lives.

Sirach 48:1-4, 9-11
Matthew 17:10-13

Don't Let The Opportunity Of God Pass You By

Opportunities come in innumerable ways but are limited in their number. Opportunities come to us in our life as a student. There is the most common track of attending school from the primary grades, into high school and finishing in college. Many other educational opportunities exist, however. There is the possibility of education through trade and technical schools. The greatest opportunity for education comes each day. By our experience and "on the job training" we learn some of the most valuable lessons, whether they are of a technical nature or more personal in their perspective.

Opportunities come in other areas of our life as well. Many opportunities are found in our lives in the working world. Offers come at various times and places. Sometimes the job offer we want comes via our use of a resume, but not always. Word of mouth spreads information that allows those in the right place at the right time to get a job. Advertisements in the newspaper provide opportunities. Sometimes the best job comes merely by passing a sign that says, "help wanted." By taking some risks in the working world we can create our own opportunities.

We discover opportunities in relationships with others. Where does one meet one's spouse — on the street corner, at a dance, a church function or possibly at school? Some of the best friends I have in my life were gained when I was in the navy. We can meet special people in many ways and different places. Opportunities come in many ways, but in a limited amount; we cannot allow them to pass us by.

God comes to us in innumerable ways, but we need to recognize God and use the opportunity effectively. As we continue to hear in our readings, today as the past few days, John the Baptist came to prepare the way for the Lord. He was thought by many to be mad; others did not listen. Today we hear that he was thought by some to be Elijah. Despite his connection with one of the great prophets of old, John was still not recognized by many. As we hear in the first reading, the wisdom literature of Sirach predicted the return of Elijah as one to prepare the way. Even with the prophecy of the Scriptures and the message of John, the presence of God in Jesus was missed. The opportunity of God came and bypassed many people.

We have the opportunity to encounter God each day, but many times we do not take the chance. As the popular motion picture from a few years back, *Dead Poets' Society*, advanced the expression *Carpe Diem* (seize the day), so we must seize the special moments and opportunities in our life. We are privileged to encounter the living God; let us not allow the opportunity to pass us by.

Like the opportunities of life, education, work, and relationships, our opportunity to find God can come in countless ways, but only in limited amounts. God can be found in all peoples and things, but we must seize the moment and take the opportunity to find God. God will be manifest in many ways. Our preparation must include our search for the living God. Let us never allow God to pass us by!

Question Authority?

People in positions of authority have a tough road these days. Parents are in positions of authority with their children and their task today is difficult. I am convinced that being a parent is the toughest job in the world. Children many times today question parents' motives in decisions which are made. Children also challenge parental rights to act on their behalf. The workplace is also a difficult environment for those who exercise authority. Employers today are forced to defend their authority in relationships with employees. The rights of employees have come to the foreground. People are afraid to act in the workplace for fear another may complain about what is done. Fear is raised when different attitudes or opinions are voiced. The Church is not immune from this problem with authority. The authority of the Pope is constantly under fire; the concept of the magisterium is under question. Bishops and pastors are many times caught in the middle between the institutional Church which they represent and the people whom they shepherd. The bumper sticker which is commonly seen on cars says it all — "Question Authority."

In the Gospel we hear how the Jewish leaders of Jesus' day questioned both his authority and that of John the Baptist. The question put to Jesus by the chief priests and the scribes was blunt and straightforward, "On what authority are you doing these things? Who has given you this power?" Jesus, as always, is too smart and clever to be trapped by his enemies. In his question and the response given by the Jewish leaders it is clear that the leaders were more afraid of the people and their view of John than they were of Jesus. They did not worry about Jesus since they did not recognize God's presence in their midst.

Balaam, whom we hear about in the first reading from the Book of Numbers, was an outsider; he was not of the company of Israel. Despite the fact that he is a foreigner, Balaam is able to see the authority of God, present in the community of Israel. Balaam recognizes the presence of God in the Israelites. He says, "A star shall come out of Jacob and a scepter shall rise out of Israel"(24:17b).

Humans question the authority of God in many ways, most of which are subtle. People may not even realize that what they do questions God's authority. We may question God by our ignorance and inattention. What role does God play in our lives? How much influence does God's presence have on what we do? Do we make time for God in our lives? At times as well we question the authority of God by our actions. We sometimes worship the created world and the creator is ignored. There are times we reject God's message and law. We conduct our lives with little thought of how our actions affect other humans, those who are God's greatest creation.

Our preparation for the Lord must place God first in every aspect of our life. The hustle and bustle of contemporary society tends to pull us away from our roots, which must be centered in God, the true vine. Let our preparations for the coming of the Lord center on our relationship with God. Let us not question God's law and authority. Rather, let us rejoice in the presence of God's loving hand which leads and guides us to where we need to go. Let us conform to the authority of God and find eternal life.

Zephaniah 3:1-2, 9-13
Matthew 21:28-32

Humbling Oneself
Before The Lord

Dorian Grey was a young and egocentric man. A friend painted a portrait of Dorian that was truly a master work of art. This painting was very special to the young man for it portrayed him with a strong and youthful countenance. Dorian liked the work so much that he actually fell in love with its image.

The youthfulness illustrated in his portrait was highly attractive to Dorian. In fact, Dorian Grey never seemed to age as the years went by. He always looked as youthful and as fit as the painting he loved so much. Dorian's ability to remain youthful while the world around him aged made him more despicable and difficult as a person.

One day after a lifetime filled with arrogance and a sense of superiority, Dorian returned home to view the portrait he loved so much. The picture had changed. What he saw frightened him greatly. The portrait was of an ugly and vile man. All the arrogance and nastiness of his life was present in the face of the portrait. Then he looked in the mirror and saw the same image in his own person. Dorian Grey would die with the tortured expression of his haughty and vile nature written on his face. In a rapid turn of events all was lost in his life.

The *Picture of Dorian Grey*, a classic story made into a popular movie in the 1930s, demonstrates how the lofty of stature can fall so swiftly. Our readings today suggest that status and position mean little before God — rather the ability to humble oneself before God is what is needed.

In the first reading we hear from the prophet Zephaniah. This man wrote to the Hebrews in Judah in the seventh century BCE,

42

before the Babylonian captivity. The Hebrews saw themselves as special people, exalted above others, including the marginalized of their own Jewish society. God warns the people through the mouth of the prophet, "For then I will remove from your midst your proudly exultant ones, and you shall no longer be haughty in my holy mountain" (3:11b). But God will not abandon the people — no, a remnant, those who are humble and lowly, will remain. These will take refuge in the name of the Lord. They will do no wrong and speak no lies.

In the Gospel Jesus warns the chief priests and scribes that prostitutes and tax collectors will enter the Kingdom of God before those who exalt their own righteousness. The meek and lowly person, the one who can humble herself before the Lord, this is the one who will find God.

Our society stresses the need to exalt oneself. Certainly a sense of personal prowess is necessary. For people today to get the job, the promotion or the position, we need to step forward and show our best effort. As my dad has always said, "You need to toot your own horn because no one will do it for you." The world is competitive and we need to enter in fully or we will be lost.

What is our attitude, however, in the way we approach the world? Many Hebrews during Zephaniah's time thought themselves better than others, especially the poor and marginalized. Jewish leaders of Jesus' time put themselves above those they considered sinners and transgressors of the law. Our attitude can never place us above another. We may be more qualified, we may have greater gifts but we are not "better" than others. We need to admit our brokenness, accept it, and then use it to better ourselves and our world. As our preparation for the Lord continues let us remember the lesson of Dorian Grey and reject attitudes that puff us up and make us seem better than others. Let us seek to humble ourselves before the Lord, open our hearts, and find peace in the palm of God's hand.

Isaiah 45:6-8, 18, 21-25
Luke 7:18-23

Proof Positive —
God Is With Us

The criminal justice system in our country uses evidence as a primary vehicle in the adjudication of a case brought before the court. Evidence is necessary as described by Scott Turow in his best-selling 1990 novel, *The Burden of Proof,* to determine the outcome of a case. Lawyers on each side of the aisle try to convince a judge or jury of a client's innocence or guilt based on the evidence presented. Evidence in any case comes in two forms. Circumstantial evidence cannot be physically displayed; it is indirect. Circumstances place an individual in a given place at a given time, yet there is no direct confirmation of this fact. Direct evidence is usually physical in nature — a person saw the incident in question; a weapon or document is presented to judge, jury, and other participants. Once the evidence has been presented a decision must be rendered: innocent or guilty. Hopefully, the evidence presented supports the case of one claimant over the other.

In Christian history there have been several academic attempts to prove the existence of God. The evidence provided was philosophical and more circumstantial. Saint Anselm in the eleventh century attempted an "ontological" proof for God's existence. In the thirteenth century the famous Dominican scholar Saint Thomas Aquinas produced another intellectual proof for the existence of God. Despite these efforts people remain unconvinced of the presence of God.

Our readings today sound like a presentation of direct evidence in a case to prove the existence of God. In the first reading Isaiah gives many examples of direct evidence for the existence of the Creator. He speaks of God as the one who formed the light and

44

created the darkness. God is the one who is the creator of the heavens and the designer and maker of the earth. We hear that only in the Lord are just deeds and power. Above all, God is the one who brings forth justice and salvation to the world.

In the Gospel the disciples of John the Baptist come to Jesus with the question, "Are you he who is to come or are we to expect someone else?" John wants direct evidence that Jesus is the one for whom the Hebrews have been waiting. Jesus gives John's friends all kinds of evidence as to his identity. Jesus tells them to report what they see to John: the blind recover their sight, cripples walk, lepers are cured, the dead are raised to life, and the poor have the good news preached to them. John, his disciples, and all of us have the evidence. What is our verdict? Is God present; is God manifest in our world?

We live in a world which seems to become more dangerous, complicated and troublesome by the year. We see darkness, that which is sin, invading our society to an alarming extent. For those of us who live in the northern hemisphere this time of year seems to verify what we feel in our hearts and think in our minds, as the days become shorter and darkness envelops our world. However, the evidence is in; the proof is positive — God is with us!

Contemporary society is fixated on problems, violence, anger — all that is the darkness in our world. Anyone who has recently watched a television newscast has experienced this morbid trend. But the Prince of Peace, the Light of the World, is coming and will break through the darkness with a magnificent display of power and goodness, wisdom and love. The metaphors of today's readings are as true today as when they were first written. The earth is good; the rains do water our world. Those who are dead in mind and spirit are raised to a new and better appreciation of life. The good news is preached to the poor and those in need of God's special care. With such positive and direct evidence we can do as God asks in the words of Isaiah, "Turn to me and be saved, all the ends of the earth! For I am God, and there is no other" (45:22).

The proof of God's presence is all around us. We can look out our window and see the evidence. The proof is positive; the verdict is in — God is with us! Let us turn to God as our preparation begins to center on the coming of God's Son in history. Let us pray that if we were ever placed on trial for being Christians there would be sufficient evidence to convict us!

The Faithfulness Of God

The concept of commitment is a many times ignored or abused idea these days. Many people simply choose to ignore and not participate in commitments. People refuse to enter into commitments, whether they be relationships, business contacts, or community activities. We feel that commitments tie us down; we feel trapped if we enter in and fully participate in any program. If we simply ignore commitments then we can go about our business with one less burden. After all, we live in a contemporary world where most of us stretch ourselves thin and are over-committed.

Commitments are abused as much as ignored. Unfortunately, the commitment which goes with relationships is regularly abused these days. Mothers and fathers are less committed to the duties associated with their children, as well as their mutual commitment to one another. Children fail in their commitments to parents and peers alike. In the business world commitment is also in serious jeopardy. Employees feel little loyalty to company or organization. Who can pay the most and provide the best benefits for the least amount of effort — this is the bottom line question for workers today. Employers use, even abuse, their employees; they make little, if any, commitment to those who work for them. Business is business; the days of the company as family are rapidly evaporating.

In the readings today we hear of the commitment of God to the Hebrew people. The second section of the book of Isaiah (chapters 36-55) from which we hear today was written to the Hebrews in exile. It sounds a strong message of promise and hope. Salvation history is the story of God with his people. It is based on a promise of mutual commitment. God will care for the people; all that is necessary will be provided for salvation. The people in turn must be loyal and obedient to God's law. The people felt abandoned by God during their exile. We hear, "For a brief moment I abandoned you … In overflowing wrath for a moment I hid my face from you …" (54:7a,8a). This passage, however, centers on the renewal of God's promise, to enlarge the nation and return the people. God says in Isaiah's words, "My love shall not depart from you, and my covenant of peace shall not be removed" (54:10b).

Saint Luke in his Gospel shows that Jesus is the culmination of salvation history. John the Baptist was sent as a messenger to prepare the way, to testify to the light. God's commitment to the people was never ignored or abused. God has always been present, despite his rejection by the Hebrews. God's commitment made use of prophets to point out the correct path, to steer the people in the proper direction. Such was the mission of John.

Commitment is difficult these days and if we are honest we sometimes do ignore or abuse this important concept. God, however, is ever faithful despite our actions. Scripture says, "If we are faithless, he remains faithful — for he cannot deny himself" (2 Timothy 2:13).

Today's readings challenge us to re-evaluate our commitment to God and God's people. Are we committed to a life of prayer and refuse to let obstacles keep us from our goal? Are we committed to a life of service and ministry, however it may manifest itself? As Christians are we committed to a life of hope and refuse to be swayed by the pessimism of society? Can we trust in God as much as God places faith and trust in us?

Walter Elliott, a well-known Paulist priest of the latter nineteenth and early twentieth centuries, once wrote of our relationship with God, "Trust that is rooted in God is a blossom on the living tree of hope, that only changes its bright leaves for the ripened seed of eternal life." As we prepare for Jesus' Incarnation let us review our commitments and make every effort to be faithful. Then we will blossom forth and experience God's promise of salvation and eternal life.

Isaiah 56:1-3, 6-8
John 5:33-36

God
Accepts All

We have all heard the expression, "Variety is the spice of life." This idea is expressed in many things we do, both the ordinary and those special times in our life. Most people seek variety in the food they eat. People who go out to dinner with regular frequency usually vary where they go and what type of food they eat. One night it is Italian; another night it is Chinese. Sometimes people return to the American standards such as meat and potatoes or fast food. There is variety in fashion. Over time styles change. Wide ties make the circuit of being in, then out, then back in fashion. Leisure suits had their day as did pump shoes, mini-skirts, and turtlenecks. We seek variety in entertainment and other special activities. We go to the movies and sometimes say, today is a time for comedy while other times we say, I want to see a drama or science fiction. Music and reading also provide great variety. Sometimes we want to listen to rock, other times jazz, and maybe still other times Beethoven, Mozart, and Tchaikovsky will suit our fancy. Reading provides mysteries, romance, biography, and many more venues.

The readings today speak about the variety which God welcomes into his house and how Jesus served to bring this message to our world. Isaiah the prophet wrote to the Hebrew people as they returned from their fifty year exile in Babylon. The prophet tells the people that salvation is about to come to the people. This salvation, however, is not exclusive to Israel. No, the foreigner, the outcast, all who hold the Sabbath free from profanation will be welcomed into God's house of prayer. Others will be gathered into the family of God besides those assembled as the nation of Israel.

Jesus, as we hear in today's Gospel, is the one who brings this message to God's people. God the Father sent Jesus for this task. The people knew of John and his special mission, but Jesus' testimony is more important. The works which Jesus performs witness to this special message.

We do say that variety is the spice of life and in some ways this is very true. We are inclusive in some things such as food, music and maybe what we read or wear. However, whether we admit it or not, we are exclusive in some very important ways. We are many times exclusive in what we are willing to do. We are afraid to venture out and try a new way, a new idea. We become set in our ways, even stubborn at times, We will not attempt something that seems to be difficult. We are also at times exclusive in our attitudes. We don't like to listen to other opinions, new ideas or what others think. We choose to believe what we believe — and that is it! We are also at times exclusive in our dealings with people. We won't associate with those who are not as smart as we wish or those who might not be attractive to us. We put people to the side because they are not of the same economic class, religion, ethnic origin, or race. This exclusivity divides and isolates us from the possibilities that other things, attitudes, and people can provide.

Jesus' message of love and peace is inclusive. It reaches to all people in its meaning and relevance. We need to be more inclusive in all that we say and do. We need to develop trust that other ideas and possibilities will strengthen us; variety is not the enemy. The defenses and barriers which we place before us may provide a shield to that which we do not want, but they also keep God at a distance. As we prepare for the newborn Prince of Peace let us include all peoples and ideas as our variety or spice of life. When we do, we imitate Jesus, the one whose presence we await!

Rooted In
The Lord

The publication of Alex Haley's prize winning novel *Roots* in the 1970s was the catalyst behind a new wave of people who sought to discover their heritage and ancestry, their roots. Investigation of one's genealogy and the generation of a family tree became commonplace. The heritage that we possess, as individuals and in our communal ethnic diversity, was brought to the forefront.

The investigation of one's heritage led to some amazing discoveries. Some people, I am sure, found that they were related to a person of importance, fame, or renown. Others, I am equally certain, discovered that they were linked in their genealogy to a name or movement which they and history would like to forget. Many people discovered relatives and relationships that they never previously knew. Many surprises were discovered along the way of determining one's roots!

Today we start in earnest our preparation for the arrival of Jesus in history. Jesus' presence is imminent; his arrival requires our immediate preparation and concern. The liturgical theme of the readings from today until Christmas center on the coming of Jesus, his Incarnation, and birth. God is ever close; we must open our eyes and recognize the presence of God among us.

As a start to this more intense preparation, today's readings describe the roots or ancestry of Jesus. Isaiah tells us how Judah will be graced among all the twelve tribes of Israel. The other eleven will bow down before Judah. The scepter will always be present with this tribe. Tribute will be brought to Judah; the people's homage will be received.

Saint Matthew, who wrote to Greek-speaking Jews and Jewish Christians, is highly interested in describing the heritage, the roots, of Jesus. Thus, unlike any of the other evangelists, he begins his account of the life of Jesus with a genealogy. Matthew wants to show that Jesus is the fulfillment of the prophecy of Isaiah. The evangelist shows that Jesus came from the tribe of Judah and the house of David. Jesus is, thus, the descendant of a king. He has the lineage to support his claim as the new King of the Jews. Jesus, as well, is a direct descendant of Abraham, the father-in-faith for all Jews. His claim to a rootedness in the heritage of his people is firm.

When we trace our roots, our ancestry, we can go only so far. Written records and memories can establish some links with the past, but we will always be uncertain as to our original origins — or will we? A little thought can easily tell us that the physical nature we have and the faith we share can be traced back to the origin of all life and good, that is to God. Physically we know that we have come from God and will one day return to God. Our faith, the Christian tradition, has historical roots. We can read about the origins of our Church in Scripture, especially the Acts of the Apostles.

With the knowledge that our physical being and faith is part of God's plan, can we claim that we are rooted in the Lord? Do we treat God with the respect deserved, both in the way we handle our person and the efforts we make to nurture our faith? Is our rootedness in God visible to others? Can family, friends, and business associates tell that God makes a difference in our lives? When we see a person we often say he looks Italian or she speaks with a British accent. Would people who observe our lives be able to say, he or she is rooted in God?

As we begin the final stage of our preparation for the coming of the Lord, let us remember the source of who we are and what we believe. Let us profess with all we say and do, in imitation of Saint Paul, "Jesus Christ is Lord, to the glory of God the Father" (Philippians 2:11b).

God Is Anything But Ordinary

We usually associate the word "ordinary" with things that are routine, normal, even mundane. Most of what we do each day can be labeled ordinary. Monday through Friday we have our routine. We wake up each morning, get dressed, throw breakfast down our throats, get into our cars, and go to work. We spend our required eight hours on the job. Then we head home, fighting the traffic along the route. Upon arrival we flip on the television, eat dinner, and then relax. Possibly we transport our child to a sports practice; maybe we take the family out to dinner. We get our six, seven, or eight hours of rest and then the routine repeats itself.

Most people long for times when the routine can be broken, times when the ordinary can be transformed into the extraordinary, the non-routine. Weekends allow some change of pace for us. Three-day weekends are even better. We wait with a certain impatience for our next vacation break. It will be a time when we can kick back and do whatever we please. There are times in the daily routine, however, when we attempt to break out: we attend a play, we listen to a concert, or we go to a ball game. The non-routine changes things and makes life more interesting.

In our readings we hear about events which usually are very common, we might say routine and thus ordinary. Yet, with God there is nothing that is ever ordinary. The Hebrew people knew from their heritage that a Messiah would be sent by God. This redeemer would be a king; they hoped he would be like the great King David. Jeremiah, however, in today's first reading suggests that the king to be sent will not be of any ordinary ilk. This king will save Judah, not from the oppression of outside peoples, but

53

from its sins. That is why he will be given the name "the Lord our justice."

This king, who will be different and special, will arrive in a very extraordinary and miraculous way. Imagine if you can the thought of Joseph when the Angel of the Lord came to him. He certainly knew the tradition of the Hebrews and the hopes of the nation of Israel. Joseph was asked to make a major "leap of faith." Mary, his fiance, is pregnant through the power of the Holy Spirit, an extraordinary event for sure. Prophecy will be fulfilled. This will not be any ordinary child nor ordinary king. He will be Emmanuel, a name meaning God is with us. Joseph may have wished for a routine and uncomplicated life. Yet, he, like Mary, accepted God's will and call in his life.

Our lives are mostly routine. Most of the things we do each day are quite ordinary. However, we have the opportunity to encounter God each day, and God is anything but ordinary. We encounter God in events, the great, the beautiful and the memorable. We also encounter God in the ordinary, routine, and mundane. We must make every effort not to miss the opportunity when God passes by. God is present in nature. God is present in the ordinary life and death of the light at dawn and dusk each day. God is also present in the power of the ocean surf and the creative force possessed by a volcanic eruption or an earthquake which changes the face of the land. God is present most especially in people. God is present in a warm smile, a caring attitude, and an ear that is willing to listen.

Each and every encounter with God, through events, nature, and people, has the possibility to be extraordinary. How God is received, however, is up to us. If we choose to see little or nothing, then God's presence may seem ordinary. However, if we look at the possibilities present, then God is anything but ordinary. We realize that Jesus, the one for whom we wait, was born in humble conditions, in what seems at first glance to be an ordinary manner. Yet, in faith we know that he came with a message and an attitude of love which can transform the world. Let us recognize the many possibilities which God presents, for to encounter God is anything but ordinary!

Judges 13:2-7, 24-25
Luke 1:5-25

Being Open
To The Possibility

The difficult we do today; the impossible we do tomorrow. I learned this expression many years ago from my high school tennis coach, Mr. Harp. This challenge was set before my teammates and me as a motivational tool. Today we might think ideas to be difficult or even impossible, but my former coach's expression says that we must meet such challenges head on. The difficult we must tackle today and the impossible tomorrow. But tomorrow will come and we cannot back away from this reality.

Coach Harp never wanted any of us on the team to let an opportunity pass by without our recognition of its presence. The tendency for us as youths (and for most people, I suspect) was to think that some things were just too difficult; there were tasks that were beyond us. Thus, at certain times we never made the effort and the opportunity was lost. Our own sense of what was possible was stunted; we limited our options and our future if we said things were impossible. When, however, we challenged what was thought to be impossible, we took the risk to believe. Many other options and possibilities then became present.

In our readings today we hear how what seems to be impossible is made reality. We hear two stories which on the surface seem very similar, but differ on several important points. In the Book of Judges we hear about Manoah and his wife. She was barren, a reality which at times was thought to show disfavor with God. In a similar way the Gospel tells us that Elizabeth, a woman who was barren and moreover advanced in years, was found to be pregnant. Both children to be born are to be consecrated to the Lord. Both were to serve as messengers, one as a judge and leader of the people, one as a precursor of the Lord.

There are important differences in the two accounts. The account in Judges says that the angel of God came to the wife of Manoah with the news of her pregnancy. Manoah does not question this rather astonishing news. Rather, he is cooperative and asks what he needs to do to prepare for this special child. In the Gospel account Zechariah is told of his wife's pregnancy. He questions the remarkable news; he is skeptical about such a possibility.

The attitudes expressed by Manoah and Zechariah are both present in all of us. Sometimes we are like Zechariah; we refuse to believe that the seemingly impossible can become a reality. We limit our options; we give only lip service to the future. We have thus aided the determination of the future by saying that certain things cannot be done. Such an attitude will only allow us to do certain things. Opportunities come into our lives and pass by; we do not even recognize what we have missed.

Many times the limits we place on ourselves keep the possibility of God's presence at bay. We may say in our head that we will do the difficult today and the impossible tomorrow, but for God tomorrow is today; God has no human time schedule. God does not limit the options for humankind; neither should we.

We are challenged to hold the attitude of Manoah. When something seems improbable we must ask,"What can I do to help make this event, attitude or possibility become a reality?" Our participation and effort makes possibilities into realities. With faith in the presence of God all becomes possible.

The coming of God into our world is a highly unlikely event. Why would God enter our world? We know the answer: God chose to come, to set us free, to lead us home. If we can believe in the impossibility of the Incarnation, then we can also believe in other ideas that seem beyond probability. Let us believe in Jesus, what he brings and the possibilities we all can share!

The Proper Receptacle For God

Jack McArdle in his book *150 More Stories for Preachers and Teachers* tells the following story: A chaplain on a battlefield came across a young man who was lying in a shell hole, seriously wounded. "Would you like me to read you something from this book, the Bible?" he asked. "I'm so thirsty, I'd rather have a drink of water," the soldier said. Hurrying away, the chaplain soon brought the water. Then the wounded man said, "Could you put something under my head?" The chaplain took off his overcoat, rolled it up, and gently placed it under the man's head as a pillow. "Now," said the suffering man, "if I just had something over me. I'm cold." The chaplain immediately removed his jacket and put it over the wounded man to keep him warm. Then the soldier looked the chaplain straight in the eye and said, "If there is anything in that book that makes a man do for another all that you have done for me, then please read it, because I'd love to hear it."

The story of the Army chaplain indicates how close God can be, especially when we recognize him in the presence and actions of others. Our readings today speak of the immanence of God as well. In the first reading Isaiah proclaims a famous prophecy. The virgin shall be with child and his name will be Immanuel, meaning God is with us. God has been with the Hebrew people from the outset and desires to continue this relationship in a more intimate way. In the Gospel, the story of the Annunciation, we hear the fulfillment of this famous prophecy. God is with his people.

Besides being a fulfillment of prophecy, the story of the Annunciation provides the perfect example of one who allowed herself to be a receptacle for the presence of God. I am sure that

Mary, like all of us, had many plans and dreams. She probably planned to marry Joseph and raise a family, a rather ordinary life for a Jewish woman. All of her ideas, however, went on hold or were changed forever with her acceptance of God's invitation. Mary was able to sense the immanent presence of God. Her fiat or yes, "Here am I, the servant of the Lord; let it be with me according to your word" (Luke 1:38a), showed her to be the proper receptacle for God. She was open and willing to respond to God's call. Because of her receptivity God made her the Christ bearer, the *theotokos*, the Mother of God.

Where is God for us? Is God out in the distance someplace or is God immanent? As we approach the birth of the Savior this is an important question to ponder. If we believe that God is near then we must be able to recognize the Lord in the simple, routine, ordinary, even mundane aspects of our lives, as well as the great, powerful, and beautiful. We must be able to recognize God in events. We can see God in the birth of a child and the joy which such a miracle brings to all. God is present in the birth of nations, the downfall of tyranny and the rise of democratic institutions. Such events have been dramatically seen recently in the breakup of the Soviet Union and the rise of Eastern European nations. God must be found in the birth of ideas which allow people to build a world community and transform society.

God must be found in nature. God is present in the birth of new bodies of land. A volcano erupts in the ocean and a new island is created. Earthquakes rock the land and create anew. God is present in the birth each day of the light at dawn and its death each evening at dusk. God is present in the serenity of a country stream and he is present in the power of the surf crashing on the ocean shore.

God certainly is present in events and nature, but if we believe God is near, then he most especially must be seen in people, like the chaplain in Jack McArdle's story. We see God's presence in others and others see God in us. Therefore, when we smile, God smiles. When we are friendly and say "Good morning," God says "Good morning." When we take the time, make the effort, visit the sick, and listen to the brokenhearted, then God takes the time, makes the effort, gives welcome, and listens.

Let us look around and see the immanent presence of Christ. Let us clear out some of the baggage in our lives and prepare a receptive spot for the newborn Prince of Peace.

Song of Solomon 2:8-14
or Zephaniah 3:14-18
Luke 1:39-45

Anticipating
The Lord

Anticipation is an aspect of life which we have all experienced. Sometimes anticipation is difficult. For example, we hear about the illness of a friend or relative and we anticipate incapacity, hospitalization or even death. Possibly the company for which we work is in financial straits and we anticipate a lay-off notice.

Most times, however, we associate anticipation with positive expectations. We look forward to things that will make life better and more worthwhile. All of us anticipate our next celebration. Who does not look forward to his birthday, anniversary or special holiday? Working people say they "live" for the next three-day weekend. We also look forward with anticipation to the completion of some project that has taken time and energy. Graduation from school and the closing of a major business deal are such anticipated events. We also anticipate arrivals. When we know that a friend, family member or associate is due to arrive we make ready for the visit. It is an event which we anticipate with joy.

In our readings today we hear of the heightened anticipation for the coming of the Lord. Both of the possible choices for today's first reading speak of the joy found in the presence of the Lord. The Song of Solomon is a love poem. This book of Scripture is often read at weddings. We hear in prophetic language how Jesus is seen as a lover whose arrival is eagerly anticipated. Like a gazelle he comes. The lover's arrival sees the winter pass. The flowers again appear on earth; the fig tree bears its fruit. The lover's voice, like that of the dove, is sweet.

The prophet Zephaniah speaks of the future greatness of Israel. The Lord will remove all judgment against the Hebrew nation.

60

The Lord will be present in the midst of the people; they will have no further tears. God will renew the people in love. God will sing joyfully over the nation.

In the Gospel we hear the well-known story of the visitation. Mary anticipated the birth of her cousin Elizabeth's child. She unselfishly made the journey which was not an easy task in those days. I am sure that Elizabeth was excited about Mary's visit, but it is her future son, John, who, while still in the womb, senses and anticipates the presence of God. The baby leapt in her womb and Elizabeth was filled with the Holy Spirit. The long awaited Redeemer and Messiah, Jesus, is near. The anticipation of Israel was at its peak.

We are in a process of anticipation in our preparation for Jesus' arrival. By now the many tasks necessary for Christmas are near completion. The gifts should be purchased and wrapped; the house is certainly decorated. The cookies, candy and other foods are prepared. We have been in preparation for almost four weeks; our anticipation is at its peak.

Our readings challenge us to anticipate the Lord, not the gifts and goodies, but rather what God brings in the Incarnation. God brings peace, love, renewal of spirit, and joy. Can we anticipate and hold on to these intangible ideas? The material things which we may receive will come and go, but the special gifts which God alone can bring are here to stay, if we so choose. As individuals and society we need to choose whether our anticipation is for one day, one moment, or for a lifetime. Let us center ourselves in anticipation of the Lord. Our preparation is near to completion. Let us persevere and continue on the road that leads to Jesus and eternal life!

I Samuel 1:24-28
Luke 1:46-56

Thanksgiving To God

Prayer, as we all know is a basic element of our Christian roots and formation. We are taught as children by our parents to pray each morning and evening. Saint Paul exhorts us in his writings to "pray constantly" (Ephesians 6:18). There are many forms of prayer. Personal prayer is something in which we engage each day. Hopefully, we have our own private prayer time and use a method that works for us. There is also liturgical prayer. There are prayer services in which people speak with God as a community.

In our personal prayer we find various methods that are helpful. Some people are good at meditation. Prayer, if it is done properly, is a conversation and any conversation goes two ways. We must listen to God as much as we speak with God. Thus, the value of meditative prayer is great. There is prayer of petition. We are most familiar with this form. When we need something we ask God. This is appropriate since Jesus himself suggested that we do it: "Ask and it will be given to you; search, and you will find; knock and the door will be opened for you" (Luke 11:9). Although not as common, there is also prayer of thanksgiving. We engage in this form of prayer most frequently when something special happens in our lives. If we pray for something specific and it is received then our voice of thanksgiving is heard loud and clear.

In our readings today we hear two famous passages which are prayers of thanksgiving. Hannah, the mother of Samuel, was thankful for the birth of her son. Samuel was to have a special mission. His mother realized this and thus, as we read, consecrated him to the Lord. Hannah prayed in thanksgiving to God for the favor that had been hers to bring forth her son into the world.

Mary's famous prayer of thanksgiving, the Magnificat, is heard in today's Gospel. Mary, like Hannah, realized the special privilege afforded her by God. She was to be the mother of the Messiah and realized that, "all generations will call me blessed" (Luke 1:48b). Mary believed that God had visited her in the presence of the Angel Gabriel. Now God was within her; she was the Christ bearer. Mary's prayer of thanksgiving is said in the presence of her cousin Elizabeth. As such it expresses the hopes of both women and their common note of thanksgiving for God's favor in their lives.

For what are we thankful in our lives? It is quite easy to express thanks for the great, grand, and beautiful in our lives. When the project is completed, the job offer is received, the sick person recovers or when we escape disaster, we naturally turn to God. How difficult it can be, however, to give thanks for the ordinary. Should we not express thanks for our lives? A friend of mine when questioned, "How are you?" many times answers, "Well, I did not see my name in the obituaries so it will be a good day!" Such an attitude expresses thanks for the gift of life. Can we be thankful for the ordinary such as the warmth of the sun and the rains which renew the earth? Most especially can we show thankfulness to the many people in our lives, especially those we see every day and thus may take for granted?

Do we give thanks for the presence of God in our life? God is always present; we can count on God. If we are not careful, however, we may see God as routine. But as we said earlier in our preparation, God is anything but ordinary or routine. As Hannah and Mary gave thanks and praise to God in their prayers, so must we never fail to be thankful for the many ways that God is manifest to us each day.

Jesus is coming soon and we must express thanksgiving for his arrival. Does the renewal of God in our hearts mean something today and will it mean something next week? Let our words and actions proclaim the greatness of the Lord. Let our thanksgiving prayer be heard this day!

The Main
Event Is Near

Most all of us have had the opportunity to attend at least one musical concert. We know there are all types of concerts including rock, jazz, country, and classical. Possibly with the exception of classical music, where a particular orchestra or artist is featured, most concerts feature a warm-up group or individual before the main attraction. This warm-up group has a particular function — to get the crowd ready for the main event. Generally warm-up groups sing the same style music as the featured artists. If the featured artist is mellow, so is the warm-up; if hard rock is to be featured, the warm-up group will be of this nature. A similar message is received from both groups, warm-up and feature, which gives consistency to the concert. The warm-up artists are gifted but their purpose is to point to the featured attraction, the person(s) with the name and/or fame.

Salvation history, as described in the Scriptures, tells the story of one warm-up person after another, who were sent to prepare for the main event, the arrival of the Messiah. The prophets, both major and minor, served as the warm-ups for Jesus. Like Malachi, from whom we hear in our first reading, the prophets gave a message which was meant to prepare the people and to point them to the Messiah when he would arrive. Malachi today says that his job is to refine the people as silver is purified in the fire. He promises that Elijah will come before the day of the Lord. He will come to make final preparations, to turn the hearts of fathers to their children and children to their fathers.

In the Gospel we hear about the birth of the last of the warm-up acts, John the Baptist, the new Elijah. After a long line of prophets who have had a message, who have pointed toward another, John is born as the final precursor to the Messiah. John's birth, like that of Samson and Samuel, about whom we have heard on earlier days, was special. He had a special mission; even his name was special. The people were frightened when Zechariah proclaimed the name John on his writing tablet and his tongue was loosed. Earlier in our Advent preparation we heard about what John did in his ministry to prepare for the Messiah and his work. Today we hear about the birth of the precursor, the final warm-up. We can be certain that the birth of the Messiah is near!

At concerts warm-up acts help to keep the people awake and their interest high. We all have a tendency to doze, whether it be at a concert, in front of the television or in our task of preparing for the Lord. It is easy to slack off when we know that the main attraction is far off and will not be seen for some time. With the birth of John we know that the final warm-up has begun. We need to return to our seats and be alert; time is drawing short. The final preparations must be made so that we can give our undivided attention to the main attraction, Jesus, who comes to us soon.

The spirit of the season tells us that Jesus is near. Our readings tell us that John, the promised Elijah, the final precursor, is here. It is time to turn our hearts and minds to Christ. Let us center ourselves in him and find the peace and joy which only God can bring!

The House Of The Lord Will Stand Forever

Anyone who has ever had the opportunity to tour Europe has been impressed with the many old and beautiful churches which exist both in the British Isles and on the continent. Many of these edifices are centuries old. When we see them we wonder how they were built — the time it must have taken, the effort, especially without modern means of machinery. The grand arches, beams, and stained glass are marvels. The furnishings, including paintings, mosaics, carved altars, and statues are wonders as well. These churches have passed the test of time. They have been accepted as permanent houses of the Almighty God. These buildings are a testament to the faith of the people who built them.

As wonderful as the churches of Europe are, they can send a false signal as to the origins and content of the Church. In the first reading today we hear about David's desire to build a special house for the Lord. David as king has been living in a beautiful house of cedar, while God has lived in a tent. He asks the prophet Nathan's advice. David learns that God is not interested in a special house. God has always dwelt with his people, his community, as an immanent God. There is no need for some special structure to house the presence of God. Instead of a house for God, the Lord will establish a house for David, a line which will culminate in Jesus. David learns that God's family is more than a building.

It is Zechariah's famous prayer, known as the Benedictus, which we hear in the Gospel, which summarizes salvation history and the roles of Jesus and John. God dealt mercifully with the ancestors of the Hebrews. God removed fear so the people could worship the one true God. Now in this age God has raised up a horn of strength in Israel, through the house of David. This is Jesus whose birth will come very soon. Jesus is the one who will lift the people from darkness and bring peace to the world. John will be the prophet of Jesus, "the Most High" God. He will go before the Lord and provide a straight path. John will give a message of salvation and freedom from sin.

We look at magnificent buildings and say, "What a beautiful church." But what is the Church? Saint Paul says in his letters that we are the Church, the Body of Christ. The buildings in which we worship are magnificent, they are testimonies to God — but they are not the Church. If there were a building but no people, the Church would not exist. However, if there were people and no building, the Church is present.

Jesus Christ is the main event, the star of the show, as we said yesterday. His birth is the beginning of something special, something for which the world has waited so long. Jesus is the promise of God as found today in his Church. Some theologians say that Jesus had no intention of forming a Church; others say that he would not recognize the Church today. The Church was started however, if not personally by Jesus, then certainly in his spirit utilizing the message he gave as recorded in the Scriptures. Jesus is waiting in the wings to bring salvation to his Church, the people of God. He is the one who can lift us from darkness and bring us peace. Are we ready to receive the gift and act upon it?

Jesus is coming and the world waits. The beautiful church buildings will collapse, but the Church which is the people of God will always stand. Let us allow the Christmas message of Jesus' birth to strengthen us in our resolve to do God's will. Our Advent preparation is concluded. Let us await with joy the new born Prince of Peace.

Discipleship:
Answering God's Call

"When God calls a man, he bids him come and die." Dietrich Bonhoeffer, the well known Lutheran theologian and pastor, wrote these words in his famous monograph *The Cost of Discipleship*. Bonhoeffer knew the reality of this statement in his own life. During the period of the Third Reich in Germany, Bonhoeffer continued to follow the Lord, to be a disciple — despite the consequences. During the late 1930s he ran a clandestine seminary, always moving and staying one step ahead of the Nazi onslaught. He wrote books, essays, and other tracts against the tyranny of Adolph Hitler's government and its policy of exterminating Jews. Eventually he was captured and in April 1945, just prior to the Allied liberation, he was executed at Flössenburg, after spending two months as a prisoner at the infamous Buchenwald concentration camp.

In these readings we hear about the life of discipleship to which all Christians are called. In the Gospel we learn about the call of Andrew, his brother Peter and their friends James and John. What was the reaction of these simple but sincere men to the call of Jesus? We are told by the evangelist that they *immediately* left their boat, their family; they left everything they knew and became his followers. These men were in a fundamental way asked to begin their lives anew. Despite the uncertainty of the future, they went without asking questions or raising arguments.

What was the task of these first apostles? Saint Paul, writing to the Christian community at Rome, says that the main task was to preach, to pass on Jesus' message of faith, hope, love, and peace to others. It was a difficult task, especially in the hostile environment in which they lived. From the tradition we know that Andrew and the other apostles, save John, paid the full price of martyrdom, the same price suggested and paid by Dietrich Bonhoeffer. The brave men and women of the apostolic age as well as our own century were able to make such a commitment because they had knowledge of the great reward offered by God. As Paul writes, "If you confess with your lips that Jesus is Lord and believe in your heart that God raised him from the dead, you will be saved. Faith in the heart leads to justification, confession on the lips to salvation."

We have all been called by name, just as the first apostles, to be followers of Jesus. This call came initially through baptism. It was a call to live in the world, but not of the world. It was a call to put Christ before all other things in our life.

Our promise is the same as those first apostles. With faith we too one day will arrive in the presence of Christ. We might not be able immediately to drop all things as did Andrew and his friends, but we must respond to our Christian call to follow Jesus and lead lives of holiness. Let us reflect on our response to the call of the Lord in our lives. Let us answer with conviction and joy. Let us be God's servants and preach the word, certain that one day, with faith, eternal life will be ours.

Genesis 3:9-15, 20
Ephesians 1:3-6, 11-12
Luke 1:26-38

Obedience — Our Opportunity To Say Yes!

Obedience, what most would define as doing what others tell you to do, seems to be in rare supply these days. We are all a bit rebellious and the free spirit of individualism is alive and well in our society. Youths many times see authority figures, whether they be parents, teachers, coaches or mentors, as the enemy. Individual freedom is threatened, we feel, when a cap is placed on our activities. Workers also do not like to be told what to do or how to do it. Many times assignments are done only grudgingly out of fear of the loss of job or position.

Obedience today seems to have a pejorative connotation. We feel that through the action of obeying another we have relinquished a personal right. People see obedience as keeping us down; our possibilities and therefore our growth is somehow stunted.

Obedience should not be a pejorative term nor should we feel restrained by it. Rather, obedience can bring special opportunities to all who are open to the possibilities that come from God. In the first reading today we hear that it was a lack of obedience which cost Adam and Eve. Every opportunity and possibility was present for them. When, however, they ate from the tree of knowledge, their innocence was lost and with it all the opportunities which God had planned for them. Obedience led to the attainment of all they could use or need; disobedience lost it all, including their future.

In the Gospel we hear of Mary's acceptance of God's invitation. Her fiat or yes to God created many possibilities for her. Mary's obedience to God's wish required that she change her own personal plans. We fail to remember that Mary was engaged to Joseph and most probably planned a normal married and family life like the Jewish people of her day. Her obedience led, however, to the Incarnation. Mary was the vehicle for this miracle which brought salvation to all of us. It is well to take note of Mary's preparation from her conception for her role as the Mother of God. God's plan for the redemption of the human race was only possible by Mary's obedience, her yes to God.

The obedience which we show can also produce many opportunities. If we are open to God's dynamic plan, then we are not restricted nor is our personal freedom limited or removed by saying yes to God. Rather, the possibilities and opportunities become innumerable when we allow God's loving plan to guide us. Mary knew this to be true in her special thanksgiving prayer to God, "My soul magnifies the Lord, and my spirit rejoices in God my Savior, for he has looked with favor on the lowliness of his servant. Surely from now on all generations will call me blessed; for the Mighty One has done great things for me, and holy is his name." May we believe and do the same!

*Reflections
for
Christmas Day*

Isaiah 62:1-5
                                           Acts 13:16-17, 22-25
                                              Matthew 1:18-25

God's Promise
And Our Response

Recognition is a concept which humans both enjoy and need. People enjoy being recognized for something that they have done. When we make a positive contribution recognition is ours. This can come from many things we do, an invention which aids society, a famous statement that becomes a "catch phrase" for many, or the service that we render on behalf of those who are less advantaged than we are. Recognition also comes when we achieve some special goal. The accomplishment of some athletic record, the achievement of a favored position in the company, or the completion of some project leads to our recognition by others. Recognition comes to the noteworthy, those who make news. It may not be news on national television. Maybe it is only news to our family, but it is news nonetheless and we recognize this fact. It seems that we must do something to be recognized; something out of the ordinary is required. Recognition, as much as it is desired and needed by individuals and society, does not seem to come without our effort.

The special message we hear in the readings for Christmas Eve is that Jesus came in fulfillment of God's promise and brought recognition to the whole world. We as a community did absolutely nothing. In the first reading we hear from a section of the book of Isaiah written during the Hebrews' return to their native land after their exile in Babylon. The people have returned to rebuild their lives and their community. In the words of the prophet, God reiterates the promise made long ago to Abraham, Isaac, and the other patriarchs. The land of Israel and its people will not be forsaken; rather the Hebrews will be called "my delight" and their land "espoused." God rejoices in Israel as a bridegroom rejoices over his bride. God chose Israel, not from any merit on the part of the people, but rather out of gratuitous love. This is the great difference in God's recognition. There is no need to do anything great or make a significant contribution. God recognizes the people for who they are and for this alone. In fact, God continued to choose the Hebrews despite their lack of faithfulness.

Jesus continues the gratuitous action of God the Father through his recognition of all of us. The culmination of salvation history in the birth of Jesus, which our Gospel and second reading describe, is the fulfillment of the promise of long ago. David's line produced the Messiah, who is the King of kings and Lord of lords. Jesus' birth is an event of joy to all in the possibilities it brings. Jesus rejects no one; rather he recognizes all people for all times.

In his coming as one of us, Jesus recognized us through no merit of our own. We, in turn, are asked to recognize others for who they are and not what they were yesterday or what they will be tomorrow. What people bring is of no significance; who they are is all that matters. Yes, Jesus asks us to recognize others. Unconditional love is when we can love people as they come to us, with their strengths and weaknesses, their gifts and their foibles. We need to recognize families, friends, and business associates. Each person is a gift to us in his/her own way. Can we take the time to see it?

God made a great promise to us, to send the Son, the one whose birth we celebrate this day. We as well have made promises to God, in little and big ways. Can we give a gift to Jesus and make good on our promises to him? The promise we made may be subtle; we may not have overtly promised God anything — at least as we best remember. But whether we realize it or not, our promise to God began at Baptism — a promise to live as God's children, a promise to ministry and service.

The fulfillment of God's promise in the Christmas event should spur us on to reconsider our own promises. Let us begin those famous New Year resolutions early this year. Let us respond to God in a special way as our gift to Jesus, the newborn Prince of Peace.

Jesus Brings The Light

Picture yourself in the forest. It is night and clouds cover the moon and stars. It is dark, gloomy, and frightening. You feel your way around in the dark. You finally remember that you brought a candle and match with you. You pull the candle from your pocket and light it, placing it on a nearby tree stump. What does one notice from the candle? First, it is obvious that the light from the candle goes out in all directions. It goes to all things at all times. The light of the candle brings warmth. It is cold in the forest and the warmth is welcome. The light of the candle gives direction. We can use the candle to find our way. The light of the candle adds clarity as well. Not only can we see the direction but we can better recognize the danger spots that might be ahead. We can see more clearly which way to go. Finally the light of the candle dispels fear. Darkness is where danger lurks; we are afraid of the dark. But the light of the candle dispels fear and brings us hope.

A couple thousand years ago the Hebrew people were in darkness. It was not a physical darkness as we experience in the forest but they were in darkness nonetheless. The light of the world was absent. Even though darkness reigned, the people had hope. Isaiah the prophet says, "The people who walked in darkness have seen a great light" (9:1). The people were waiting for the light to enter the world, the one whom they would call "wonder-counselor, God-hero, Father forever, Prince of peace" (9:5b). Thus, with the arrival of the promised one, the Christ, light entered the world.

Jesus, the light of the world, came, as we hear in the famous account of Luke the Evangelist. He brought what the light of the candle brings. First, he brought himself which is none other than

77

love. The love of Christ, like the light, goes out in all directions to all peoples for all times. Nothing can escape from the love of Christ as Saint Paul tells us in his letter to the Romans (8:35-39) except the person who refuses to accept God's love. The light which is Jesus brings us warmth. If we are hurting, sorrowful or in need of comfort, it is the light of Christ which gets us by. The light brings assistance for any and all of our needs. The light of Jesus brings us direction and clarity. Guided by the Lord we know better which way to go and we are better able to avoid the pitfalls and detours which hinder our progress back to God, the one from whom we came. Finally, the light of Christ brings us hope while dispelling fear. Jesus, the light, does this by rekindling the spark of faith, a faith given us by God. Fear is dispelled by faith, not by courage or bravery. The light which is Jesus brings everything that the light of the candle brings but more, for Jesus is the light of the whole world.

Jesus' birth is for us a message of hope. Jesus did not have to come to our world; he chose to come. Jesus did not have to become human; he chose to become human, like us in all things but sin. Jesus did not have to redeem us; he chose to save us from all things including ourselves. Jesus was born one time that first Christmas day. What we celebrate at Christmas is the rebirth of light into our world. With Jesus not physically present it might seem difficult to see the light. Thus, we are challenged to become the light, the Christ, to others. We must bring love where none exists. We must bring warmth where sorrow reigns. We must be willing to give direction to others. We must dispel fear and raise hope. Let us bring love, warmth, and direction to others this Christmas. Let us rekindle the light of the Lord in our lives and share our warmth with others. Let the spirit of Christmas live in our hearts today and each day of our lives.

What Is Your Gift For Jesus?

It was Christmas evening and Monsignor Flanagan, the pastor of St. Patrick's Parish, was in a dither. The statue of the Baby Jesus was missing, apparently stolen from the crib. Who would do such a thing, especially on Christmas Day? Such was the downside of an otherwise beautiful day in the parish. The Christmas Masses had been celebrated beautifully. The choir was in rare form; the church was full. Even the homily was well received. As always the people had been very kind to those in the rectory. The house was filled with food, not to mention invitations, cards, and good wishes.

That evening, however, as he toured the parish grounds before locking up for the night, Monsignor Flanagan felt something was wrong, but he could not put his finger on it. Then he saw it, or more correctly, he didn't see it; the statue was missing. He called his young assistant, Fr. O'Connor, and asked if he knew anything about the missing statue, but he knew nothing. Fr. O'Connor did, however, agree to help look. The two priests searched high and low, with no positive results. They decided to make a few phone calls. First Fr. O'Connor called the police, but there had been no break-in or problem reported; they knew nothing. Then the call went to Patsy Mullin, the President of the Parish Council. She had been at home with her family all day and knew nothing about the missing statue. The two priests could think of nothing else to do. They locked the church with the hope and a prayer that the statue would be returned.

The next morning, after a restless night of sleep, Monsignor Flanagan woke early. About 7:30 he went to unlock the church to prepare for the morning Mass. As he scurried about the sacristy preparing for the Eucharist, he heard the front door of the church open and with it a clanging sound of wheels. When he peered out the sacristy door the pastor saw little Johnnie Murphy, the eight-year-old son of John and Mary Murphy, prominent members of the parish. Johnnie was not alone; behind him he pulled a brightly painted new red wagon. When Monsignor Flanagan looked more closely, however, he noticed that there was something in the wagon. There, wrapped in a blanket, was the statue of the Baby Jesus. Johnnie wheeled his load to the front of the church and then parked the wagon. He proceeded to take his precious passenger and place it in the crib where it belonged. The pastor approached the young man and said, "Johnnie, did you take the statue of the Baby Jesus?" The boy quite forthrightly said, "Yes, I did." "Why, son?" continued Monsignor Flanagan. "We have been looking all evening and were quite worried." The boy answered, "Well, you see, Father, I prayed all Advent for a red wagon and when it showed up on Christmas Day I was sure since it was Jesus' birthday that he should receive the first ride." Yes, little Johnnie Murphy received a special gift, one which he wanted very much. He realized, however, where the gift ultimately came from and the need to respond.

Our readings on Christmas morning speak to us about the events we celebrate, but they also tell us about the gifts which Jesus brought and our need to respond. Both Isaiah and Luke the Evangelist tell us about the events we celebrate. Isaiah speaks in a prophetic voice, "Say to daughter Zion, 'See your salvation comes' " (62:11b). Luke describes the events as reported to him. The passage we hear this morning is a continuation of the midnight reading. We now hear that the shepherds have arrived at the place of Jesus' birth. They begin to understand the message of the angel. They are in awe at the sight and give thanks and praise to God for what they have seen and heard.

As well as describing the events of Christ's birth, the readings more importantly tell us about the great gift which Jesus brought and our challenge to respond. Again, Isaiah speaks in a prophetic voice. God will come with reward and recompense. God has chosen the Hebrew people — they are a people uniquely God's own. They will be the redeemed of the Lord. It is Saint Paul in his letter to Titus, however, who gives us the information we need concerning this great gift of redemption. We hear that the gift was given, not from any merit of our own, but simply out of God's mercy and gratuitous love. It is Jesus as well who brings us the new birth of baptism. The Holy Spirit will come and through his presence we will be justified by grace, become heirs of hope, and inheritors of salvation.

Christmas is a time of joy, a time for family, and a time as well to exchange presents. It is the custom in our country to give and receive gifts. Some people open their gifts on Christmas Eve and some on Christmas Day. We give gifts out of love. All of us like to receive gifts; we would be less than honest if we said anything else. Most of us as well like to give gifts. We are all familiar with the expression, it is better to give than to receive. But to whom do we give our gifts? Certainly we give gifts to members of our family, close friends, and maybe a business associate or good neighbor. Do we, however, like Johnnie Murphy think of giving a gift to Jesus? After all, isn't it our custom to give gifts to the one whose birthday we celebrate?

What might be our gift to the newborn King of the Jews? Possibly our gift is one of greater attention, attention to God and to God's people, especially the alien, sick or less educated, those who exist on the fringes and margins of society. Maybe we can give the gift of prayer, with the promise that nothing will come between this most important commitment between ourselves and God. Can we give the gift of ministry, both in the community and in the Church? Possibly our gift is one of peace, in our own hearts and minds as a start and then branching out to society as a whole, as a welcome to the newborn Prince of Peace.

Yes, Jesus has come to our world. He chose to be like us in all things but sin. He also chose to give us the great gift of salvation so that we could be with him forever. On this Christmas Day let us think about what our gift might be to Jesus, and let us give it with the same fervor as Johnnie Murphy gave the first ride in his wagon to the Lord. May we give our lives to Jesus; may the Christmas message change us forever.

Christmas Day

Isaiah 52:7-10
Hebrews 1:1-6
John 1:1-18

Accepting The Lord Once Again

He came softly, unobserved and yet, strange to say, everyone knew him. The time was the fifteenth century; the place was Seville in Spain. He came to announce peace and to proclaim the good news. He came to teach and to cure; he came to bring the light. As he walked by the cathedral, a funeral procession for a little seven-year-old girl was just beginning to form. He heard the sobs and pleas of the girl's mother. Moved with compassion he asked the bearers of the funeral bier to halt. He touched the girl; she was raised to life once again.

The local cardinal heard about this event. Such displays of power were not to be tolerated. Such action led to faith which would only be dashed in the cruelty of the world. He was thus thrown into prison as a common criminal. In prison he was questioned by the chief or Grand Inquisitor of the city, "Why have you come? We don't need you here!" The prisoner made no response. The Inquisitor thus continued his harangue. He questioned the prisoner about his time in the desert, at the beginning of his ministry, when he was tempted with the great luxuries of power, wealth, and prestige. "You were a fool," said the Inquisitor. "You should have accepted Satan's offer! Why are you so bent on self-destruction? Why did you choose miracle, mystery, and authority over power, wealth, and prestige? There is no longer a need to believe in you and what you bring. Go away, you are not welcome here." This time the prisoner did answer, not with words, but with actions. He embraced the Inquisitor, kissed him, and walked out of the prison. He moved on to offer himself to another group at another time in history.

82

Fydor Dostoyevsky's famous chapter, "The Grand Inquisitor," in his book *The Brothers Karamazov* describes the rejection of Christ who has come to bring light, goodness, and peace to a world who needs him but refuses to accept his presence. In a similar way our readings on Christmas Day speak of what Jesus brought to the world and how he was rejected.

Isaiah writes to the Hebrew people in exile in Babylon. The people have little hope; they live with the thought that they have been rejected by God. However, Isaiah prophesies a new beginning for the nation. This new life for the people will restore Zion. The Lord will come to the people announcing peace, bearing good news, comforting the people, and announcing salvation. The Lord will thus provide all that the people need to renew their lives and live as God's people.

In the Letter to the Hebrews Jesus is described as the reflection of God's glory. Jesus is the one who is exalted far above the angels. Jesus brought his powerful word to our world, a word which sustains those who believe in him.

John 1:1-18 is one of the most famous passages in Scripture. Possibly more has been written about this pericope than any other. We are told by John that Jesus was the Word made flesh; he is the presence of God who dwells among us. Jesus was the light, a favorite metaphor of Saint John's writings, a light which no darkness can overcome. Jesus, the Son of God, brought his message of salvation, hope, and love.

Today we celebrate the feast of Christmas. It is the Incarnation, the coming of Jesus, the one who is the light, the Son of God, into our world. Jesus came and we rejoice in this fact. But we know the end of the story as well as its beginning. Jesus was rejected by the very people to whom he came. Saint John says today, "He came to what was his own, and his own people did not accept him" (1:11). Have things changed that much in 2000 years?

We look at our world and wonder if the Prince of Peace has made any progress in his struggle to find acceptance from the greatest creation of the Father, the human race? Thousands starve in Somalia because the light is not accepted. Violence eclipses peace in our streets. Ethnic cleansing is what the Serbs call their atrocities against Muslims in Bosnia-Hersgovina. Racial tensions continue to plague South Africa and make international news. Where is the good news? Where is the comfort and salvation of God?

With all the problems and bad news we may wonder what significance Jesus' birth in Bethlehem has for us today. The answer is totally up to us. An event which happened almost 2,000 years ago must be applied today in order to find relevance and meaning! If we do nothing to make Jesus' presence meaningful for our world, then like the Grand Inquisitor, Christ's rejection will continue. Jesus brought hope; he brought light so that a people in darkness would never be fearful again. It is up to us!

John Michael Talbot, composer, singer, and author, puts the challenge before us by borrowing from Saint Teresa of Avila. "Christ has no body on earth but yours, no hands, no feet but yours. Yours are the eyes through which Christ looks with compassion for the world. Christ has no body on earth but yours." As the prayer indicates we are the presence of Christ. We are the light, the hope, the bearers of Good News. If Jesus' birth means something more than a respite from the day-to-day grind then it must take root and blossom forth in what we say and do. As Saint Paul says, we are the Body of Christ. We have a responsibility to pass on the gifts Jesus brings to others. We begin with ourselves and then move to others.

There is a painting in the British National Gallery in London. It describes in art a passage from the Book of Revelation, "I am standing at the door knocking; if you hear my voice and open the door, I will come in to you and eat with you, and you with me" (3:20). Let us today respond to the knock of Jesus; let us open the door to our hearts. Let us welcome the newborn Prince of Peace. Let us allow the miracle of Jesus' birth to change us forever!